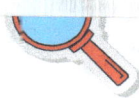

TEACHER

© 2024 Julie Dascoli

All rights reserved. No part of this book may be reproduced or transmitted in any form or by any means, electronic or mechanical, including photocopying, recording or by any information storage and retrieval system, without prior permission in writing from the publisher.

Published in 2024 by Amba Press, Melbourne, Australia.
www.ambapress.com.au

Previously published in 2015 by Hawker Brownlow Education.
This edition replaces all previous editions.

ISBN: 9781923116900 (pbk)
ISBN: 9781923116917 (ebk)

A catalogue record for this book is available from the National Library of Australia.

TEACHER

Written by Julie Dascoli

Photography by Laura Dascoli

Dear Reader,

Welcome to this volume of the *Real People Real Careers* series. I hope you'll enjoy learning all about Sarah and her work as a kindergarten teacher.

Before you read on, I'd like to say a few thank-yous to the people who helped to make this book possible.

Firstly, thank you to Laura Dascoli, who took the photographs you see in the book, and to Donna Dascoli, who provided initial editing and computer support services.

Secondly, my thanks to the staff and students in Years 4, 5 and 6 of the Mossgiel Park Primary School class of 2015 for their unwavering help and support.

And finally, I'm grateful to Sarah herself, who generously gave up her time to help others learn about her profession – and to show them all the ways in which her job rules!

Happy reading!

Julie Dascoli

TEACHER

My name is Sarah and I'm a teacher. During my teenage years, while I was visiting a very sick cousin, I decided that working with children was the career I wanted to pursue. After I finished Year 12 at my local high school, I attended **TAFE** to do a **diploma** course. I wanted to work in a **childcare centre** and look after small children.

My **TAFE** course took two years of full-time study. I studied subjects like **child development**, music and movement, and children with **additional needs**. Upon completion of my course, I was qualified to work in a **childcare centre**.

I found a job at a local **childcare centre**. The centre was divided into rooms according to the ages of the children. I worked in the three-year-old room and the babies' room. Some of the children were there every day – five days a week – while their parents went to work, so I formed a special bond with them.

After working at the **childcare centre** for two years, I was offered a job as a **nanny**. A **nanny** is employed by a family to take care of their children at their home. It was a nice change to work one-on-one with a child in a family setting.

I had been employed by the family for half a year when I found out that the parents were going to work in America for six months. They invited me to travel with them and continue to care for their child. I felt very lucky to be able to work and see another country at the same time.

Upon returning to Australia, I continued to work part-time for this family, and I found a job with another family as well. During this time, I began a **university** course called a **degree** so that I could become a kindergarten teacher. I felt like this was a natural progression from what I had been doing.

The **TAFE** course that I had already completed allowed me to do the **degree** in two years instead of four. It was a busy time for me, especially as I got married and had my two children during the same period. However, it was very rewarding when I finally completed my Bachelor of Early Childhood Studies. I am now a kindergarten teacher.

It was time to start looking for a job. I applied by email for a kindergarten teacher job with my local council. Within a few days, I was granted an **interview**. They asked me a lot of questions about myself and how I work. They also allowed me to ask questions about the job. After waiting for a few weeks, I received an email to say that I had a job starting in the following year. I was so excited that all my hard work had paid off.

PAGE 4   REAL PEOPLE · REAL CAREERS

When I'm teaching, I like to have several types of drawing mediums available for the children, such as coloured pencils, felt markers and paint. It is beneficial for the children to practise applying both heavy and soft pressure to make a mark. It is also good for them to experiment with mixing colour, which is possible with paint. I also keep a supply of differently textured materials – such as fabric, twine, buttons and boxes – so that the children can create three-dimensional constructions using these materials and their imaginations.

Together with the children, I grow seasonal vegetables in planter boxes. We plant them, water them, and when they are ready to pick, we cook or prepare them in some way so that the children can experience the journey of healthy food.

I also keep stick insects in the classroom. It's educational for the children to observe and care for the insects as they hatch from their eggs and grow into adults.

Tasks I perform every day

- → When I arrive at work, my first job is to set up the classroom and the outside play area.

- → As part of my preparation, I put up reminder notices for families regarding any special events due to take place during the day.

- → I then greet my staff and discuss with them anything that is likely to have an impact on the day ahead.

- → Next, I greet the families and children in my class. I make sure that all children's names are signed in the class sign-in book, as this is a legal requirement.

- → I begin by helping the children to settle in to various activities, both inside and outside the classroom.

- → I write down **observations** of the children to guide the planning of future activities.

- At some point in the day, I conduct 'group time', which can involve songs, stories, 'show-and-learn' activities and so on.
- I supervise snacks and lunchtime, and I dismiss the children at the end of the day.
- Every day I do general administrative tasks, including paperwork, photocopying, emails and phone calls.

Interesting facts about my job

- I work nine hours a day.
- I have lunch with the children.
- I can have up to 26 children in a class at one time.
- We do gardening with the children, growing sunflowers and cucumbers.
- We use the produce from the garden to do cooking with the children.
- We strongly encourage the children to recycle.
- My favourite task is to witness the development of the children.
- My least favourite task is saying goodbye at the end of the year.
- It is compulsory for me to do a **first-aid** course each year.

lockers for the children's possessions

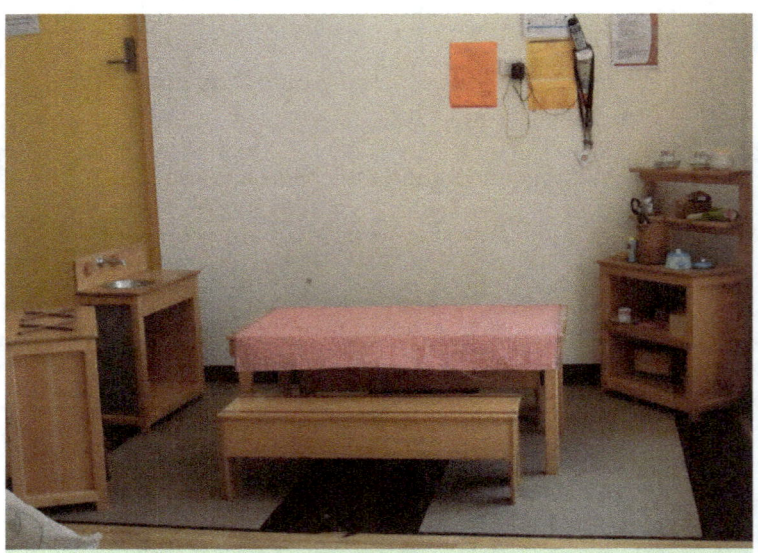

the 'home corner', where the children play make-believe

What I wear to work

I don't need to wear a uniform when I go to work. However, I do have to wear professional clothing that is also comfy, as I quite often need to sit on the floor or move freely with the children. I must wear closed-toe shoes to protect my feet.

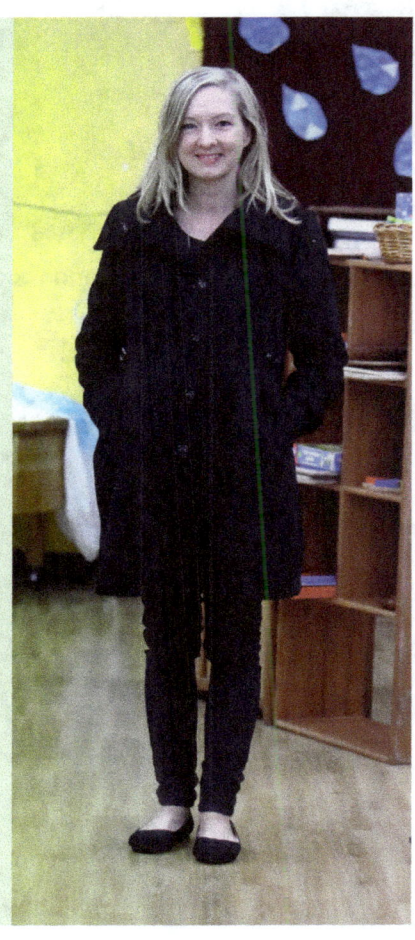

> I do have to wear professional clothing that is also comfy, as I quite often need to sit on the floor or move freely with the children. I must wear closed-toe shoes to protect my feet.

rubbish and recycling bins

outdoor climbing equipment

As we play outside in all types of weather, I need a warm coat, and sometimes a hat and gloves if it becomes very cold. In summer, I must wear a sun-smart hat, sunscreen and a top that covers my shoulders.

We play outside in all types of weather

What you need to do my job

- → You enjoy the company of small children.
- → You have a creative mind.
- → You have a patient personality.
- → You can work in a team.
- → You are an organised person.

Related occupations

- → kindergarten assistant
- → **additional needs** assistant
- → school teacher
- → childcare worker with Certificate III or a **diploma**
- → **nanny**

Postscript

Sarah is now the teacher-in-charge at the kindergarten where she works. It is a very busy job with many responsibilities, but she enjoys it very much. This is her dream job.

Glossary

Additional needs When a child is born with, or acquires through illness or injury, challenges that require additional support in an educational setting. *Sarah works with both mainstream children and children with **additional needs**.*

Childcare centre A facility where children can be cared for on a casual basis – for instance, one day per week or several hours per day – according to an agreement between the centre and the child's parents. *Sarah decided to work at a **childcare centre** after visiting a very ill cousin in hospital.*

Child development The physical, emotional and psychological growth of a child from birth to the teen years. *Understanding **child development** is a very important part of Sarah's job.*

Degree A qualification obtained at **university** upon completion of a course. *A **degree** often takes four years, but Sarah was able to finish hers in two because she had already completed a **diploma**.*

Diploma	A certificate awarded by an educational institution to prove that a person has completed a course. *Sarah completed a course at **TAFE** and achieved her **diploma**.*
First aid	Emergency treatment that is given to an injured or sick person. *All kindergarten teachers must maintain a current **first-aid** certificate.*
Interview	The process in which an employer who wants to hire a new staff member meets with a person who has applied for the job. The employer asks questions of the applicant, and the applicant can also ask questions to work out if they are the best person for the job. *Sarah had an **interview** with a local council to try and get a job as a kindergarten teacher.*
Nanny	A person who works in a private home as a carer for one or more children within that home. You can be a live-in **nanny** or a daytime **nanny**. *Sarah worked as a **nanny** for a family and travelled to the United States of America with them.*

Observations	When a kindergarten teacher watches what the children are doing and records it on paper. This allows the teacher to understand what the children enjoy doing and how they are developing, helping the teacher to plan activities for the future. *Sarah and her staff take down **observations** of the children periodically during the session.*
TAFE	A vocational school where people can learn the technical skills they need to do their jobs and earn a certificate or **diploma**. *Sarah did a course at **TAFE** to obtain a **diploma** qualification that enables her to work in childcare.*
University	A tertiary education facility where students can obtain a **degree**. *Sarah went to **university** to become a qualified kindergarten teacher.*

Other titles in this series

 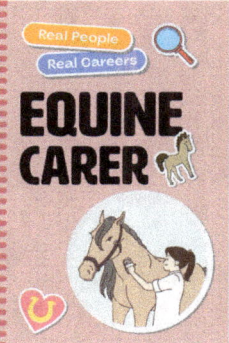 

  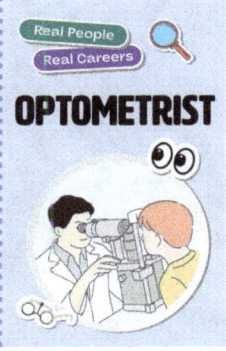

TEACHER PAGE 19

www.ingramcontent.com/pod-product-compliance
Lightning Source LLC
Chambersburg PA
CBHW070343120526
44590CB00017B/3001